Made in the USA
Monee, IL
30 July 2021

74620883R00066